LADYBUGS

LADYBUGS

by Sylvia A. Johnson

Photographs by Yuko Sato

A Lerner Natural Science Book

Lerner Publications Company ▪ Minneapolis

Sylvia A. Johnson, Series Editor

Translation of original text by Chaim Uri

Additional photographs by: pp. 5, 31 (lower left), 45, Jerome Wexler; p. 28, Isao Kishida

The publisher wishes to thank Jerry W. Heaps, Department of Entomology, University of Minnesota, for his assistance in the preparation of this book.

The glossary on page 46 gives definitions and pronunciations of words shown in **bold type** in the text.

LIBRARY OF CONGRESS CATALOGING IN PUBLICATION DATA

Johnson, Sylvia A.
  Ladybugs.

  (A Lerner natural science book)
  Adaptation of: Tentōmushi / by Yuko Sato
  Includes index.
  Summary: Describes the life cycle of ladybugs, from egg through larva and pupa to adult, and explains how ladybugs aid humans by feeding on insect pests.
    1. Ladybirds — Juvenile literature. [1. Ladybugs. 2. Beetles] I. Sāto, Yūkō, 1928-   . Tentōmushi. II. Title. III. Series.

  QL596.C65J73   1983   595.76'9   83-18777
  ISBN 0-8225-1481-8 (lib. bdg.)

This edition first published 1983 by Lerner Publications Company.
Text copyright © 1983 by Lerner Publications Company.
Photographs copyright © 1978 by Yuko Sato.
Text adapted from LADYBUGS copyright © 1978 by Yuko Sato.
English language rights arranged by Kurita-Bando Literary Agency for Akane Shobo Publishers, Tokyo, Japan.

International Standard Book Number: 0-8225-1481-8
Library of Congress Catalog Card Number: 83-18777
  5 6 7 8 9 10 92 91

Most people have mixed feelings about the 800,000 kinds of insects that share our world. Everyone appreciates the beauty of butterflies and moths, but no one has a good word to say for pesky flies and mosquitoes. Bees and wasps are admired for their nest-building skills but feared because of the painful stings they can inflict. Farmers and gardeners wage constant war against the many hungry insects that make a living by eating crops and garden plants.

But there is one insect that is on everyone's popularity list—admired for its attractive appearance and appreciated for its contributions to human life. That insect is the ladybug.

When the temperature rises to about 15 degrees Celsius (59 degrees Fahrenheit), ladybugs become active.

Ladybugs are beetles, members of a very large group of insects. They are closely related to other familiar beetles such as the shiny, black June bugs that buzz around lamps or the fireflies that light up the dark of a summer night.

Like all their insect relatives, ladybugs are **cold-blooded** animals. Their body temperatures are controlled by the temperatures of their surroundings. During cold weather, ladybugs **hibernate**, resting quietly, but when the temperature rises, they become active. The warm weather and longer days of spring bring ladybugs out of their hiding places, ready to continue the cycle of their lives.

6

Dogtooth violets (right) and other spring wild flowers make their appearance at the same time that ladybugs come out of hibernation (below).

Left: Aphids on the stem of a rose bud. *Opposite:* This black-and-orange ladybug is busy eating its favorite food.

When they become active in spring, the first thing that ladybugs do is look for food. Most kinds of ladybugs are **carnivores,** or meat-eaters, and their favorite food is a tiny insect called an **aphid.**

Aphids are soft-bodied insects that feed on many kinds of plants. They have tube-shaped mouths that they use to pierce plant stems and suck out the juices. Adult ladybugs have mouths with strong jaws well suited for chewing up aphids. By consuming these **herbivores,** or plant-eaters, ladybugs take in the important nutrients manufactured by green plants.

Above: A ladybug's strong jaws can easily crush the soft body of an aphid. *Left:* Ladybugs and aphids on a rose plant.

On warm spring days, large numbers of ladybugs gather on plants where aphids are feeding. The little beetles come to find food, but they may also have the opportunity to find a mate.

A pair of ladybugs mating. The male is behind the female.

Along with eating, mating is the main occupation of adult ladybugs. Guided by their instincts, male and female ladybugs seek partners so that they can carry out the important job of reproduction.

Like most animals, a ladybug can mate only with another individual of its own particular **species,** or kind. Male and female ladybugs of the same species recognize each other by smell rather than sight. They use their **antennae,** the short, slender sense organs on their heads, to identify the special odor produced by members of their species.

After finding appropriate partners, ladybugs usually mate on the leaf of a plant. In mating, the bodies of a male and female ladybug are joined, and **sperm cells** pass from the male's body into the female's. When the sperm cells unite with the **egg cells** in the female's body, a new generation of ladybugs comes into existence.

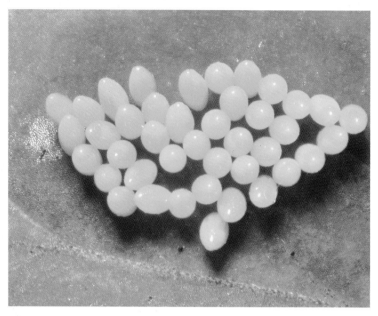

Above: A cluster of ladybug eggs. *Opposite:* Female ladybugs lay their eggs on plants where aphids can be found. The picture in the circle, taken through a piece of glass, shows eggs passing out of a female's body.

About a week after she has mated, a female ladybug is ready to lay her eggs. The eggs come out of her body through a kind of tube called an **ovipositor,** located at the end of the abdomen. They are bright yellow, oval in shape, and very small—about 1.5 millimeters (1/25 inch) long.

The female deposits her eggs in groups on the leaves and stems of plants. She is careful to choose plants where aphids live because the little creatures that will emerge from the eggs will be aphid-eaters, just like their parents.

12

These ladybug larvae are hatching from eggs attached to the underside of a leaf.

Several days after they were laid, the bright yellow ladybug eggs turn white. This is a sign that they are ready to hatch. Soon the soft shells of the eggs break open, and tiny creatures with long legs and hairy bodies begin to emerge. These little animals are ladybug **larvae.**

Unlike many other young animals, ladybug larvae are not miniature versions of their parents. In fact, they look nothing at all like adult ladybugs. Instead the larvae represent just one stage in the complicated process of development that produces adults of their species. This process, known as **metamorphosis,** is common in the insect world. In addition to beetles, many other kinds of insects—for example, butterflies, bees, and ants—go through several different stages of development before they become adults.

When the yellow ladybug eggs turn white, they are ready to hatch.

Above: Ladybug larvae emerging from their eggs. *Left:* After the larvae have hatched, their color gradually changes from white to black.

A ladybug larva eating an aphid

Although they do not look at all like adult ladybugs, the larvae have one thing in common with their parents. They have a great appetite for aphids.

As soon as they hatch from their eggs, the larvae go in search of food. Moving quickly on their three pairs of jointed legs, they scramble over plant leaves and stems. When a larva finds an aphid, it uses its sharp jaws to crush the insect's soft body and then sucks out the juices.

A ladybug larva spends most of its time eating, and it can consume enormous quantities of aphids. The larvae of some species are known to eat up to 500 aphids in one day!

There is a good reason for a larva's enormous appetite. The larval stage is the only period of growth in the ladybug's life. During this time, the insect will become at least four times bigger than it was when it hatched from the egg. After the period of larval growth is completed, the ladybug will not get any bigger.

A ladybug larva has a kind of suction disc on the last segment, or section, of its body (right). The larva uses this useful feature as an extra leg when it is crawling over plant leaves and stems (below).

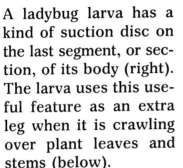

A ladybug larva molting. After the second molt, an orange pattern appears on the larva's body.

Like other insects, the ladybug larva grows in a special way. Its body increases in size, but the material that covers it does not expand.

The outer covering of an insect's body is called an **exoskeleton.** As the name suggests, this tough covering serves as an outside skeleton, protecting the internal organs and providing an attachment for muscles, just as bones do in the bodies of other animals. Unlike bones, however, the exoskeleton does not grow along with the insect's body. Therefore it must be replaced from time to time.

A ladybug larva replaces its exoskeleton by **molting.** Attaching itself to a leaf or branch, it wriggles out of its old covering. Underneath is a new, larger exoskeleton that has already formed. The larva will continue to grow until it fills out this new covering. Then it will molt again.

Most ladybugs molt three times during their larval stage. At the end of the larval period, they will shed their exoskeletons once more, but this time something very special will happen.

18

Right: These larvae are in the final stage of their development. They have such fierce appetites that they will try to eat each other if nothing else is available. *Below:* A ladybug larva on the stalk of a barley plant.

When a larva sheds its exoskeleton for the fourth time, it enters another stage of metamorphosis. Under the old larval covering is a new form of the ladybug, called the **pupa**.

Above: These pictures show a ladybug larva becoming a pupa. After finding a sheltered spot, the larva attaches the rear end of its body to a leaf or stem with a sticky liquid (1). About two hours later, the larva's skin begins to split down the back (2). Soon the larval skin is completely discarded, revealing the orange-colored pupa that has developed beneath it (3). Over the next few hours, the soft pupal shell becomes hard and a pattern of black marks appears on it (4, 5, 6).

A ladybug pupa
attached to the
stem of a flower

Just as the larval stage is one of activity and growth, the pupal stage is a time of rest and transformation. During this period, the body of the larva will change into the more complicated body of an adult ladybug.

When a pupa is disturbed, it jerks its body to try and frighten away a potential enemy (right).

The adult body parts of the ladybug are present in the larval stage, but they are undeveloped. During the pupal stage, the development will be completed, and the worm-like larva will be transformed into a winged adult with its round body and familiar spotted markings.

The pupal stage lasts about five days, and during this time, the pupa remains very still. Firmly attached to a branch or leaf, it is capable of very little movement. If it is disturbed, the pupa can twitch its body to try and frighten away a potential enemy. But most of its energy must go into the tremendous development that is taking place inside it.

As the pupa develops, the wings and other adult body parts can be seen under the pupal shell. It will not be long before the adult ladybug is ready to emerge.

A pupa can also make slight movements in order to regulate its body temperature. This pupa has raised its body to change the amount of sunlight falling on it. At the point where the pupa is attached to the tree, you can still see the discarded larval skin.

Five days after it entered the pupal stage, the ladybug has completed its development. Now it has become an adult, the final stage in its metamorphosis.

The sequence of photographs on these two pages shows an adult ladybug emerging from its pupal shell. To prepare for emergence, the ladybug first stretches out its body inside the shell (1). Soon the shell splits open along the back, and the ladybug's head emerges (2). A few minutes later, the ladybug pulls its whole body out of the shell (3). About 12 minutes have passed since the insect first began to move inside the pupal shell.

The newly emerged ladybug is a pale orange color with a very light pattern of two dots. Its true colors will not develop until several hours later.

As the ladybug moves slowly away from its empty pupal shell, it begins to extend two transparent wings at the end of its body (4).

(5)

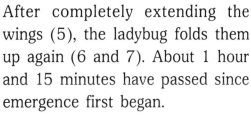

After completely extending the wings (5), the ladybug folds them up again (6 and 7). About 1 hour and 15 minutes have passed since emergence first began.

For several hours after it emerges, the ladybug is unable to fly and its body is very soft. If it is threatened by an enemy like this assassin bug (below), there is little the ladybug can do to protect itself.

(6)

(7)

These two pictures show the colors gradually developing on a newly emerged ladybug.

As the newly emerged ladybug rests quietly, its body begins to harden and its true colors develop. The pale orange gradually darkens to black, and two large orange spots take definite shape.

This particular ladybug belongs to a species that is usually characterized by two orange or red spots on a black background. Other kinds of ladybugs have different combinations of colors and different numbers of spots. There are red or gold ladybugs with black spots ranging in number from 2 to at least 28. There are jet black ladybugs with red, orange, or gold spots. Some ladybugs have spots that blend together to form strange and beautiful patterns.

On the opposite page are pictures of some ladybugs with unusual patterns and colors. Each species is identified by its scientific name.

26

Left: *Rodalia limbata.* Center: *Rodalia cardinalis.* Right: *Chilocorus kuwanae.*

Above: *Propylea japonica.* Right: *Aiolocaria hexaspilota.*

This brightly colored ladybug is a very common species. It usually has seven black spots on a red background. The beetle's scientific name, *Coccinella septempunctata,* describes its color and markings. *Coccinella* comes from a Latin word for red, while *septempunctata* means "seven-spotted."

Looking at a ladybug's colors and pattern of spots is one way to identify the species it belongs to, but it is not a very reliable method. Even within one species, there can be variations in colors and markings. For instance, the two-spotted ladybug shown going through emergence in this book belongs to a species known for its different markings.

The pictures on the opposite page show some representatives of this species, which is identified by its scientific name *Harmonia axyridis.* As you can see, the group includes black ladybugs with two red spots (1), four red spots (2), and many red spots (3). It also includes an individual with black spots on a red background (4).

Scientists believe that such variations within a species are probably caused by differences in temperature, humidity, and other conditions during the early stages of metamorphosis. In order to identify a ladybug's species, it is necessary to look at many other individual characteristics in addition to colors and spots.

The main parts of a lady-bug's body are hidden under its shiny spotted coat.

No matter what kind of markings they have, all adult ladybugs are very much alike in their general physical make-up. Like other insects, ladybugs have three main parts to their bodies—the head, thorax, and abdomen.

A ladybug's head is equipped with several useful sense organs—two antennae, which are sensitive to smell and touch, and two **compound eyes.** Also located on the head is the ladybug's mouth, which includes two sets of jaws used to seize, hold, and chew food.

Connected to the thorax, the middle section of the lady-bug's body, are two pairs of wings and three pairs of legs. The last section of the body is the abdomen, containing the organs of digestion and reproduction.

If you look closely at a ladybug, you can usually see its small head, but the thorax and abdomen cannot be seen unless you turn the beetle over. The top surface of these two body parts is completely concealed by the shiny polka-dot covering that makes a ladybug so easy to recognize. If you look carefully at the pictures on the next few pages, you will see that this spotted shell is actually the first pair of the ladybug's wings.

Right and below: A ladybug's hairy, jointed leg is equipped with two tiny claws. The last few joints of the leg also have sticky pads of hair that enable the ladybug to cling to smooth surfaces.

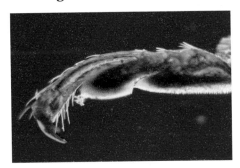

Above: A ladybug uses its front legs to clean its antennae and the other parts of its head. *Right:* This ladybug has both pairs of its wings extended.

Above: In order to fit under the protective front wings, a ladybug's back wings must be folded up in a complicated pattern. *Opposite:* This highly magnified photograph shows the fine hairs that cover the back wings.

Like all its beetle relatives, a ladybug has two pairs of wings that look very different and serve different purposes. The curved front wings, made of a smooth, tough material, form a covering or sheath for the transparent back wings. This characteristic has given a name to the scientific order to which beetles belong. It is called Coleoptera, which means "sheath wing."

When a ladybug is at rest, its back wings cannot be seen because they are folded up under the protective front wings. The front wings, known as **elytra,** meet in a neat straight line down the middle of the beetle's back. Grooves along the edges of the elytra lock them firmly together.

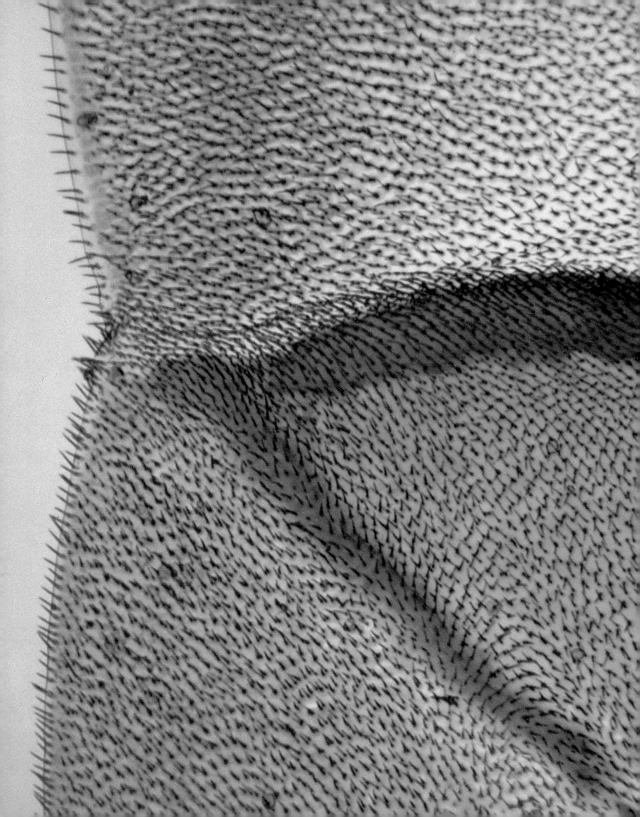

When a ladybug is ready to fly, it unlocks its elytra, raises them, and unfolds the pair of wings hidden underneath. In flight, these long, thin back wings beat up and down, moving the ladybug through the air. The elytra do not move during flight, but they help to provide lift, something like the wings of an airplane.

Compared to some insects, ladybugs and their beetle relatives are not outstanding fliers. Their top speed is about 15 miles (24 kilometers) per hour, whereas dragonflies can reach speeds of 60 miles (96 kilometers) per hour. Since ladybugs search for their food on the ground rather than in the air, swift flight is not really necessary to their way of life.

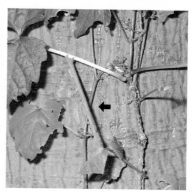

The caterpillar of a swallowtail butterfly (left) and an adult cicada (center) have colors that blend in with their surroundings. The long, thin moth caterpillar in the picture on the right looks exactly like a tree twig.

Many insects use flight not only to hunt for food but also to escape from animals that want to make a meal out of them. Slow-moving ladybugs cannot easily escape from birds and other **predators.** The bright colors of the little beetles would also seem likely to attract the attention of animals looking for food.

Other kinds of insects blend in so well with their environments that they are difficult to see. The green butterfly caterpillar shown above matches the bright green of the leaves around it. The cicada in the middle picture has grey wings and body that blend with the color of tree bark. These insects are well camouflaged against discovery by predators.

Ladybugs cannot use camouflage to hide from predators, but their colors do play a part in their self-defense. The bright reds, yellows, and golds that ladybugs wear serve as **warning colors** that tell predators to stay away.

A ladybug's bright colors stand out against the green of a barley plant.

Left: If a predator gets a taste of the bitter orange fluid that oozes from a ladybug's leg joints, it will lose its appetite for ladybugs. *Right:* A ladybug also discourages predators by folding up its legs and playing dead.

Predators will be warned away by a ladybug's colors only if they have already tried to make a meal of ladybugs. Any bird that seizes a ladybug in its beak quickly discovers that the bright-colored beetle has a very unpleasant taste.

When a ladybug is frightened or disturbed by a predator, an orange-colored liquid automatically oozes from the joints of its legs. This fluid is actually the ladybug's blood, and it has a bitter taste. A bird that gets a sample of it will begin to lose its appetite for ladybugs. Whenever the bird sees another bright-colored little beetle, it will remember the unpleasant experience and eventually learn to stay away.

This ladybug is caught in a spider's web, but the spider seems to know that its captive would not make a very tasty meal.

Ants are not usually among the predators of ladybugs, but the two kinds of insects are natural enemies. This is because both ladybugs and ants love aphids.

Ants appreciate aphids because of a sweet liquid that the insects produce as part of their digestive process. This liquid, called **honeydew**, is a favorite food of several kinds of ants. They like nothing better than licking up honeydew as it is discharged from the aphids' bodies (above).

When ants and ladybugs are feeding on the same group of aphids, there is a definite conflict of interest. To prevent their food source from being eaten up, the ants try to drive the ladybugs away by biting them with their sharp jaws. The ladybugs defend themselves by curling up and tucking their heads and legs under their hard elytra.

Ladybugs spend the winter hibernating in spots where they are sheltered from wind and cold.

Even if an adult ladybug is not killed by a predator, it usually lives only three or four weeks. During the warm days of summer, the ladybug population is constantly being renewed by new generations of adults that have developed from eggs and gone through metamorphosis. As autumn approaches, however, the adult ladybugs alive at that time stop producing eggs. The brisk autumn wind carries a message that winter is not far off, and the little beetles must prepare for the change of seasons.

During the winter months, adult ladybugs hibernate in protected places, under fallen leaves and logs or in rock crevices. Some kinds of ladybugs form large groups and fly together to a particular hibernating spot, where they spend the winter huddled in a red-and-black heap. Other ladybugs stay in their home territory and hibernate alone or in small groups.

On days when the winter sun is especially warm, ladybugs may come out of their protected hiding places and move around a little in the pleasant warmth. But they will not resume their active lives until the days lengthen and the spring flowers bloom once again.

Right: A group of ladybugs resting on their journey to the place where they will hibernate for the winter. *Below:* Ladybugs hibernating together in a rock crevice.

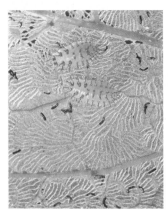

Both the larvae and the adults of this ladybug species *(Henosepilachna vigintioctomaculata)* feed on the leaves of plants in the potato family.

When ladybugs emerge in spring and make their appearance on the leaves and stems of plants, gardeners, farmers, and orchard owners are glad to see the little beetles. They know what a tremendous service ladybugs perform for humans by eating aphids and other destructive insects.

Ladybugs are considered so useful as a method of insect control that they can be purchased by the boxfuls to put into gardens and farm fields. The ladybugs are collected during cold weather, when they are hibernating in large groups. They are kept under refrigeration until it is time to release them in the fields. As soon as the ladybugs warm up, they go to work eating insect pests.

There are a few species of ladybugs that eat plants instead of protecting them from other insects. These **herbivorous** ladybugs usually feed on the leaves of bean, squash, and potato plants as larvae and as adults. They can do considerable damage to crops, but the trouble they cause is far outweighed by all the good done by their hungry, insect-eating relatives.

GLOSSARY

antennae (an-TEN-ee) — sense organs on the heads of insects, used for smelling and touching. The singular form of the word is **antenna**.

aphids (A-fids) — soft-bodied insects that live by sucking juice from plants

carnivores (KAR-nih-vors) — animals that eat meat

cold-blooded — having a body temperature the same as the temperature of an animal's surroundings

compound eyes — insect eyes made up of many tiny lenses

egg cells — female reproductive cells

elytra (eh-LIE-truh) — the hard front wings of beetles, which serve as covers or sheaths for the back wings. The singular form of the word is **elytron**.

exoskeleton — an external framework that supports and protects an insect's body

herbivores (ER-bih-vors) — animals that eat plants

herbivorous (er-BIH-vor-us) — plant-eating

hibernate — to spend the winter in an inactive state during which all body functions slow down

honeydew — a sweet liquid produced by aphids as a by-product of their digestive process

larvae (LAR-vee) — the second stage of metamorphosis, in which the insect is wingless and worm-like. The singular form of the word is **larva**.

metamorphosis (met-uh-MOR-fuh-sis)—the four-stage process of development that produces an adult ladybug and many other adult insects. The four stages are egg, larva, pupa, and adult.

molting—shedding an old exoskeleton to make way for a new one

ovipositor (oh-vee-POS-ih-tur)—a tube at the end of a female insect's abdomen through which eggs pass out of the body

predators—animals that kill and eat other animals

pupa (PEW-puh)—the third stage of metamorphosis, in which the larva changes into an adult insect. The plural form of the word is **pupae,** pronounced PEW-pee.

species (SPEE-sheez)—a group of animals or plants that have many characteristics in common. A species is the smallest group in the system of scientific classification.

warning colors—colors on an animal's body that warn predators to leave them alone

INDEX